Dedication

I dedicate this book to my heart horse, Red.

Thank you Red for taking me on our wonderful
journey. I could not have done it without you.
And I am so honored to share your incredible story
in human words.

Love, Bea

Red The One-Eyed Horse

Printed Book: ISBN 979-8-9857060-1-7
Ebook: ISBN 979-8-9857060-0-0

First edition April 2022.

One day, Bea went to visit a farm.

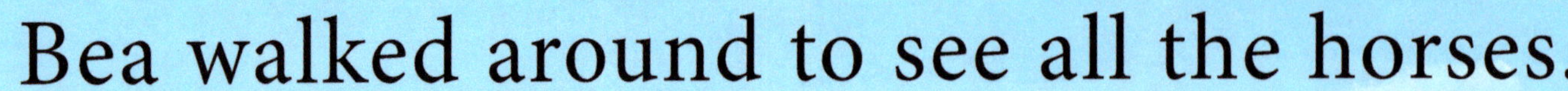
Bea walked around to see all the horses.

Bea heard a loud noise. She was curious to find out where it was coming from.

Bea saw a big brown horse playing
with a red bucket.

She walked up to the big horse and stood outside the fence. Bea decided to call the horse Red.

Bea saw that Red only had one eye.
He was missing his right eye.

Suddenly, Bea heard someone yell, "Don't get near him! He's dangerous!"

Bea did not listen because Red was kind.
She did not feel scared.

Bea placed her hand on Red's nose. She started to pet him. Red was gentle and moved closer to her from behind the fence.

Bea began to open the fence. From a distance, she hears someone yell, "He'll run out! Be careful, he is dangerous!"

In her heart, Bea knew that Red was not dangerous. She did not feel scared because Red was kind.

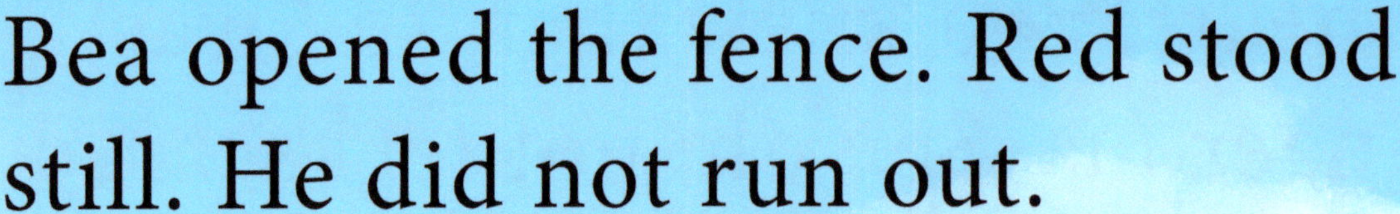

Bea opened the fence. Red stood
still. He did not run out.

Bea walked closer toward Red. She stared into his big brown eye.

Bea was not scared that Red only
had one eye. She did not think of
him as any different from the other
horses.

Red gently laid his head on
Bea's shoulder and softly neighed.
He was kind.

The next morning, Bea went back to the farm.

A boy was pointing and laughing at Red. He yelled out, "This horse only has one eye!"

22

Bea heard this and went up to the boy.

Bea puts her box of hair brushes on the ground. She said to the boy, "His name is Red. Red is kind and he is just like all the other horses."

The boy says to Bea, "I think Red is scary. The other horses all look normal, but Red does not."

She says to the boy, "Look at me and look at yourself, we look different right?" The boy thinks about what Bea says.

Bea continues to say, "I look one way and you look another, but am I scary to you?"

The boy shakes his head. He says, "No, you are not scary at all. You look different, but I am not afraid of you."

Bea takes the carrot from her pocket and feeds it to Red. She says to the boy, "Even though Red only has one eye, he is kind to me and I am kind to him."

Bea opens the gate and walks in. She gets on the stool and begins to brush Red. The boy watches as Bea cares for Red.

The boy grabs a brush from the box. Seeing that Red is not so scary anymore, he walks in. The boy says to Bea, "Here, let me help you. I think Red likes to be cleaned."

Red was happy. He loved the attention. Red shakes and his tail knocks Bea's brush from her hand. Together they laugh, both say, "Red!"

NEIGH!

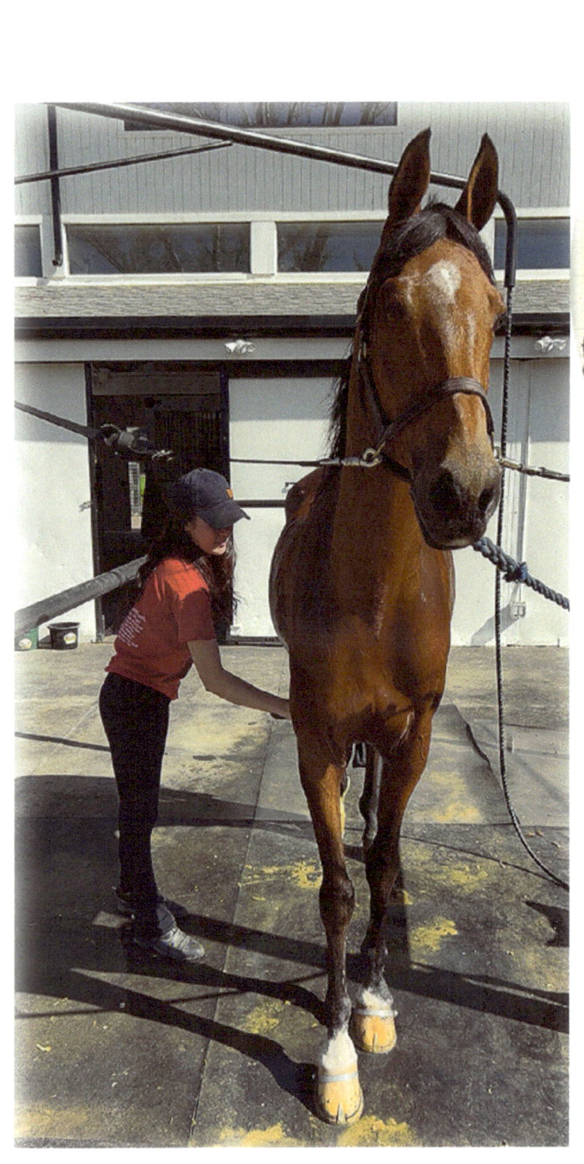

Bea & Red